Dolly's Imber

Dolly's Imber

Adapted from *Seven Miles From Any Town*

First published 2013
Revised edition 2015

Typeset by Rebbeck Cards
Design by Rebbeck Cards

ISBN 978-1517558697

Dolly's Imber

Gordon Lewis

Other titles by Gordon Lewis

Limb and Blood – the story of a Wiltshire family
(Bedeguar Books 1995)

Imber Then & Now
(Createspace Publishing 2015)

Introduction

"Little Imber on the down, seven miles from any town" reads the old rhyme in one of its many variations and it was this isolation that would lead to the fateful evacuation shortly before Christmas 1943.

I remember being fascinated by a photograph of St. Giles' Church that was published in a local newspaper during the 1970s and, despite having no known family connection with Imber myself at that time, I felt myself strangely drawn to this real life ghost village.

Yet it would be more than a decade before I finally visited the village with my future mother-in-law, Dorothy "Dolly" Hollyoake, who had spent nearly ten years living at 10 Church Street, Imber.

It is her memories that made Imber more than a deserted village, for Dolly had the ability to make the village live again as she recounted her memories to my wife, Ann, who carefully noted what was said.

Gordon Lewis
Summer 2013

Little Imber on the Down
Seven miles from any Town
Sheep bleats the only sound
Life 'twere sweet with ne'er a frown
Oh let us abide on Imber Down

Traditional

Dolly's Imber

Dorothy Amy Rebbeck, as she was born in 1914, moved to Imber with her parents and six brothers and sisters shortly after the end of World War I. The family would see another four children added to it in the years that followed, with three of these baptised at St. Giles' parish church. The small cottage, just down the hill from the church, was certainly crowded, although the older children had started to leave home by the time the younger ones came along. Nonetheless, everyone had their duties to perform and Dolly would often speak about emptying chamber pots and cleaning the front door step, before getting dressed, dressing her younger siblings and making the short walk to the village school.

Dating from the early 1920s, five of the eleven Rebbeck children are featured in this iconic group photograph of Imber Church School.

Taken almost ten years before Dolly's family arrived at Imber, the lady with her three children is stood on the steps of 10 Church Street which would later become home to the Rebbeck family.

Dolly loved her time at Imber Church School, as it was officially known, and, together with brother Frank and sisters Hilda, Winifred and Violet, is featured on the school photograph that has often been reproduced in various books about Imber and Salisbury Plain. Under the direction of Miss Burgess, Dolly excelled in all her lessons and on 31st March 1922, at the end of the old school year, she was rewarded with a certificate which confirmed that she was "industrious, made good progress, and was regular in attendance in school". Signed by Rev. Glanfield, who had overall control of the school, this certificate would become one of Dolly's most cherished possessions throughout her lifetime.

Every Sunday Mrs Rebbeck would march her children up the small hill to St. Giles' three times so that the family could attend morning service, afternoon Sunday School and Evensong at night. Dolly enjoyed hearing the Bible stories that were so vividly read by Rev. Glanfield and would proudly collect her weekly attendance stamp that was carefully placed in the accompanying album. One such album from 1926/1927 survives, in which it is noted that Dolly was unable to attend the additional Epiphany service on 6th January 1927 due to illness. Another memento from Sunday School days was a pocket Gospel of St. John with the inscription "Dolly Rebbeck for good behaviour at Imber Sunday School 1923".

Although the Rebbeck family were strictly Church of England, there was also a Baptist chapel in the village and sometimes Dolly would attend there with her mother. Although she considered the non-conformist congregation to be "chapel ranters", Dolly

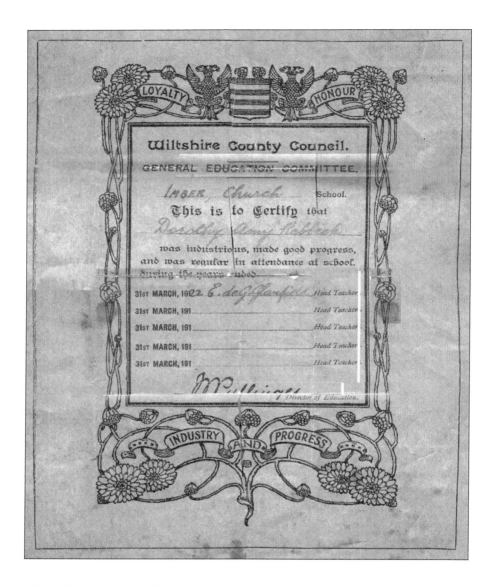

Dolly's school certificate, awarded by Imber Church School on 31st March 1922, remained a treasured possession throughout her lifetime. The original is now very fragile having been frequently handled for almost a century.

could not help but enjoy the food served at various celebratory tea parties throughout the year. Further parties were often held at Imber Court for the children of the village, but Dolly was more interested in looking out for the rumoured ghost of a white rabbit that supposedly ran between the manor house and the nearby village cricket pitch!

Imber Court

When Rev. Glanfield left the village in 1924 Dolly, like many others, was saddened by his departure. However, the ten year old girl made sure that she was going to meet the new vicar and, on the day of his arrival, waited for him by the bridge that ran over a stream near the bottom of Church Street. When Rev. Ernest Imrie-Jones finally arrived, Dolly escorted him back to the vicarage and his new home. Having been the only person to greet the recent arrival, Rev. Imrie-Jones never forgot Dolly's simple act of care, kindness and welcome.

Like all rural villages, Imber had several farmers

Each child attending Sunday School at St. Giles' Church would receive a Bible-themed stamp which was then affixed on the corresponding page of the accompanying album. Additional stamps were issued if the children attended liturgical services, including Epiphany and Maundy Thursday.

living in the vicinity, including Mr Hooper and Mr Dean who were both seen as being somewhat stern to a young girl. Then there was the kindly Albert Nash, the village blacksmith, who was loved by all who knew him and reputedly died of a broken heart after the evacuation of 1943.

Mrs Carter was the village postmistress, ably assisted by her two step-daughters, one of whom, Daisy, married Dolly's uncle, George Rebbeck. But it was Dolly's married Aunt Flo' who caused a stir following her own arrival at Imber. Within weeks she had fallen in love with the local policeman and, in order to avoid the ongoing scandal, Flo' eventually fled to Canada!

Imber Post Office

Apart from church services and the occasional village tea, there was little to do in Imber, although the charabanc would arrive once a year and take the Sunday School children to Weston Super Mare or sometimes Bournemouth for their annual seaside outing. Otherwise there was the reading room, a few

Few photographs of Dolly's parents, William Johnson Rebbeck and Winifred Clara Rebbeck (nee Drake), have survived. The one reproduced here dates from 1920 and is believed to have been taken in the garden of their Imber cottage located in Church Street.

doors away from Dolly's Imber home, where children's games would be played from time to time.

The men of the village would spend their time drinking at The Bell, but Dolly was content in making her own amusement aided by her creative imagination. With no toys to play with, Dolly would use a sauce bottle wrapped in a blanket as a doll, with the hair made from pieces of old string. On warm summer days she would sit on the grassy bank outside her home and play with a collection of stones that became her imaginary flock of chickens.

The Bell Inn

Despite ongoing military operations that surrounded the village, the young Dolly experienced little interference from the outside world and, even when that did happen, it was usually in the form of the Fish'n'Chip van which visited the village most Saturday's. Sometimes a van selling sweets would also arrive, complementing the selection that was always available at Mrs Wyatt's grocery shop near the Baptist Chapel. Otherwise the village was relatively

Another keepsake from Dolly's Imber childhood was the pocket Gospel of St. John that was awarded for "good behaviour at Imber Sunday School".

self-sufficient, with fruit and vegetables grown on the nearby allotments.

In 1925, having reached the age of 11, Dolly transferred from Imber Church School to the larger senior school more than seven miles away in Warminster. She found that to be a frightening experience, leaving the security of the close knit village for the first time, and it wasn't helped when she arrived at her new school and discovered two rather large and very scary stuffed crocodiles hanging from the ceiling of the school hall! Every day Dolly longed to return home to the security and safety of Imber.

Salisbury Infirmary

Eventually Dolly would have to leave Imber forever and, like many other girls of her age, she entered into service at the age of 14. In the six years that followed she would work for a farmer near Broad Chalke and polish the floors at Salisbury Infirmary with a piece of machinery that was almost as big as she was. Dolly then moved south to Hampshire, where her parents had also relocated, meeting and marrying Robert Henry Hollyoake with whom she would spend more than 70 years of married life. One of her younger sisters, Violet Mabel Rebbeck, would marry Robert's brother, George Frederick Hollyoake.

Although many miles now separated Dolly from Imber, she never forgot the village that held so many memories for her, and shared the anxiety of her Uncle George, Aunt Daisy and cousin John Rebbeck when they received notice to leave their Imber home never to return. George Rebbeck was already away serving in the Royal Navy, but the evacuation still affected him in ways that it is now difficult to understand. The villagers thought they were doing their duty and that Imber would be restored to them, but the War Office,

Dolly pictured outside St. Giles' Church in 1961, accompanied by her mother, Winifred, and twin daughters, Gillian and Ann Hollyoake.

which clearly had other ideas, undoubtedly betrayed them.

When greater public access to Imber was granted in the 1960s, Dolly ensured that she always returned whenever possible, taking children and grandchildren with her as the years passed. On entering the ranges Dolly would begin to recount about the different people she remembered, wondering who else would be present at the annual service and, perhaps more reflectively, who might have died during the intervening 12 months. Dolly made her last visit to Imber shortly before her 90th birthday in 2004 and, determined as she was, insisted on walking to the church unaided as she had as a child. One year later she had been looking forward to visiting once again, but became ill a few days before making the annual pilgrimage.

Dolly died on 20th February 2006, but her memories of Imber continue to live in the minds of all who met and knew her.

Dorothy Amy Hollyoake (nee Rebbeck) is buried in the graveyard adjoining St. Matthew's Church, Netley Marsh, Hampshire near her parents and Imber-born sister, Cynthia Sarah Theodora Margarretta Smith (nee Rebbeck).

In addition to her annual pilgrimage each September, Dolly also attended a special seasonal service held on 3rd January 2004 to mark the 60th anniversary of the evacuation of Imber in December 1943. Dolly was joined by three of her grandchildren, Kevin, Sarah and Rebekah Lewis, who are also pictured here.

WITH its windows all boarded up St. Giles—the church without a congregation, waits for its twice yearly visitors at the ghost village of Imber on Salisbury Plain.

But the old church had quite a few surprise tourists the other day—hundreds of soldiers from all over the world stopped off to look at the village and its church during a NATO exercise which has just finished on the Plain.

Villagers were turned out of Imber in 1943 and not allowed to return after the war. The hamlet was evacuated to provide realistic street battle training for American Forces before D-Day.

After the war the villagers took their fight to return to the House of Lords but lost. Now Imber is part of the Army's training ranges.

Twice a year the Army, who regularly maintain the church, organises a cease-fire on the Plain so former villagers can return to Imber. "Echo" photo, Pat Brookes.

The original Southern Evening Echo article that captivated the author when it was first printed during the 1970s. Almost a decade later, he would visit Imber for the first time when he was accompanied by Dorothy "Dolly" Hollyoake (nee Rebbeck) to whom the village meant so much.

Final Thoughts

Dolly had made that newspaper picture very real in the years that we had visited Imber together, and I felt honoured to have someone who loved and knew the village so well as my mother-in-law. And yet, through my own family line, I have now discovered another connection with Imber that had been overlooked until recent years.

Like any child, I am sure that Dolly would have sometimes become bored while attending the church services and probably started to look at the various memorials that still remain in St Giles' Church. One memorial is to Thomas Ayliff (sic) who had married Elizabeth Gawen, the sole heiress of Imber Court in the early 17th century. Recognising the name of Ayliffe, I soon discovered that Thomas was the half brother to my 10x great grandmother, Elizabeth White (nee Ayliffe).

Unfortunately I will never know if my mother-in-law ever looked at the memorial of Thomas Ayliffe and wondered who he was. She could certainly not have imagined that her daughter would one day marry his 11x great nephew more than 350 years after Thomas Ayliffe, one time Lord of the Manor of Imber, had married Elizabeth Gawen in the village that Dolly treasured more than any other she ever lived in.

Even so, I am sure she would have been more than a little pleased to have known of this unexpected co-incidence!

GL

Did Dolly ever look at this memorial to Thomas Ayliff (sic) located within St. Giles' Church and wonder who he was? Even if she did, she could not have imagined that one of her daughters would eventually marry Thomas's 11x great nephew!

Picture Credits:

Copyright Control; pages 8, 11, 13, 15, 21

Estate of Dorothy Hollyoake; front cover, pages 7, 10, 14, 12, 16, 18, back cover

Gordon Lewis; pages 17, 20, 23

Made in the USA
Charleston, SC
16 November 2015